GUN RIGHTS

INTERPRETING THE CONSTITUTION

— PHILIP WOLNY —

ROSEN
PUBLISHING®

New York

For Amanda Kelsey at San Loco

Published in 2015 by The Rosen Publishing Group, Inc.
29 East 21st Street, New York, NY 10010

Library of Congress Cataloging-in-Publication Data

Wolny, Philip, author.
Gun rights : interpreting the Constitution/Philip Wolny. — First Edition.
    pages cm. — (Understanding the United States Constitution)
Includes bibliographical references and index.
ISBN 978-1-4777-7516-5 (library bound)
1. Firearms—Law and legislation—United States—History—Juvenile literature. 2. Gun control—United States—History—Juvenile literature. 3. Firearms ownership—United States—Juvenile literature. 4. Firearms owners—Legal status laws, etc—United States—Juvenile literature. 5. United States. Constitution. 2nd Amendment—Juvenile literature. I. Title.
KF3941.W59 2015
323.4'3—dc23

                                          2013038827

Manufactured in China

CONTENTS

Bushmaster rifles are displayed on May 4, 2013, at the National Rifle Association's annual convention in Houston, Texas.

On a Friday morning, December 14, 2012, twenty-year-old Adam Lanza shot and killed his mother at their home. He then drove five miles (eight kilometers) to Sandy Hook Elementary School in Newton, Connecticut, where he used his mother's Bushmaster rifle to kill six teachers and other adult staff and twenty children between the ages of six and seven, injuring dozens more. There had been other worse mass shootings, but the age of the victims and the school setting attracted nationwide and international attention. Gun control supporters were furious. They felt people could obtain deadly weapons far too easily.

On December 18, four long days after the massacre, the National Rifle Association (NRA), the nation's largest pro-gun rights organization and one of the most powerful American lobbies, finally released a statement about the Sandy Hook massacre. The NRA's opponents and critics—those favoring stricter gun control laws—had attacked the organization for its silence after the event.

The NRA responded that it had stayed quiet out of respect for the victims and their families. Now, it declared its readiness to help in any way it could to prevent similar tragedies in the future. But the NRA had very different ideas about how lawmakers and the nation itself should respond to such episodes of gun violence.

Rather than ban certain weapons—such as high-powered assault rifles like the Bushmaster—or restrict their sale, the NRA suggested that schools should ramp up security, allowing for teachers and other staff to be armed. It also asserted that cases like Sandy Hook represented a failure of the nation's mental health system, rather than the perils of inadequate gun laws.

Perhaps most important, the NRA stood strong on its main point and its defining principle—that excessive regulation of any kind of firearm violates the Second Amendment of the U.S. Constitution, one of the rights explicitly outlined as part of the Bill of Rights (the first ten constitutional amendments that outline personal freedoms, states' rights, and the limits of government power).

It is precisely the Second Amendment itself that has fueled the battle over the place guns should or should not have in American life. It has often been a bitter struggle, with the NRA and its allies on one side facing off against gun control and gun victims' advocates on the other.

The political fight over the "right to bear arms" has raged among politicians and in the courts since the beginning of U.S. history. The nature of the struggle has evolved with changing times and shifting social and political contexts. The world of 1788 was very different from modern times. As long as people lose their lives to everyday gun violence—whether it is from crime, suicide, accidents, or the all-too-common rampages of disturbed shooters in public places—the gun control and gun rights debates will rage on. How the Supreme Court and other jurisdictions have interpreted gun rights in the past and will interpret them in the future will play a huge part in deciding how central a role guns will continue to have in American life.

CHAPTER ONE

GUNS IN REVOLUTIONARY-ERA AMERICA

The struggle over gun rights and gun control began even before the nation's founding. From the earliest colonists battling Native Americans for territory in the New World to white Southerners preventing freed slaves from obtaining firearms in the nineteenth century, and from increasingly easy access to modern firearms for hunting, personal security, and self-defense to tragic gun violence, it has been a divisive issue, a debate as explosive as firearms themselves.

Since the Newtown massacre, news outlets estimate that as many as 16,500 Americans have lost their lives to guns, including suicides. This is more people than American service people who perished during the nine years of the Iraq War. Thousands die every year as the result of hunting accidents, accidental shootings, and gun violence associated with crimes, disputes, and domestic incidents. Gun control advocates demand that their lawmakers address this steep toll exacted by gun violence and mishaps.

A DIFFERENT TIME

When Americans fought to free themselves of British rule in the late eighteenth century, issues surrounding firearms were very different. Americans had rebelled against the British for many economic, cultural, and political reasons.

The thirteen colonies that would unite in rebellion to form a new nation had relatively small populations and were ruled by the British Crown. Each colony had its own laws. The role of arms in daily life was a given. Colonists struggled over territory and resources with the Native Americans who had populated the New World when Europeans first arrived and required firearms for protection. Colonists routinely hunted for daily sustenance. Communities were isolated, and the long distances over which any news, warnings, or armed troops had to travel made colonists vulnerable to attack. Being armed in order to defend the community or colony from attack was a civic duty expected of all male colonists, like voting or paying taxes. Disputes with neighbors or enemies were always

This 1867 painting by George Henry Boughton, *Pilgrims Going to Church*, shows armed churchgoers.

possible, and central authorities could rarely respond in time to protect someone or respond to conflicts. Personal gun ownership seemed a necessity in these circumstances.

Denying a universal right to bear arms would have been viewed as outlandish and irresponsible. Of course, slaves, freed slaves, and Native Americans living among the colonists were often denied this right just the same. Still, the right to bear arms was very closely held by Americans long before they were Americans and long before the citizens of the new nation ratified the Constitution.

COLONIAL-ERA MILITIAS

Just before the American Revolution, there was no national or professional military force. Each colony was instead protected by local militias—often ragtag groups of citizen and volunteer soldiers. Even after General George Washington and the Continental Congress established a federal fighting force to wage war against British forces and the four main branches of the military—the army, navy, air force, and marines—evolved over the next two centuries, local militias continued to exist. In recent times, groups called "militias" have been closely associated with antigovernment and racist agendas.

This Revolutionary War reenactment in Colonial Williamsburg, Virginia, is a reminder of how closely Americans' historical identity is linked to guns.

emerged about the motivation behind the amendment and about the role of militias and who would arm them. These inspired much argument and still affect today's gun debate.

Firearms technology today is light-years ahead of eighteenth-century weaponry. Semiautomatic and automatic assault rifles are far more lethal than muskets and single-projectile muzzle-loading rifles. The urgent need for self-defense has waned with the development of professional military and law enforcement organizations. The U.S. Armed Forces, including the army, navy, air force, coast guard, and national guard, have supplanted the militias of yesteryear. Meanwhile, professional police forces exist in every small town and big city.

At the time of the ratification of the Bill of Rights, people from all walks of life owned rifles and pistols. Today, most law-abiding people in cities are not armed. Guns are largely banned, except in special cases. Nevertheless, cities like Chicago suffer from gun violence, largely because of crime, especially the drug trade. On the other hand, outside of major cities, hunting and sport shooting remain among the most popular activities in the United States.

The battle over gun rights today is dominated by two extremes, with many different opinions ranging between those two poles. One side believes that any

President Lincoln appointed Civil War veteran Major General Daniel E. Sickles to assess African Americans' plight in the South during Reconstruction, where he was South Carolina's military governor.

preventing the escape and revolt of African Americans. Along with groups of former Confederate troops, these old militias formed new vigilante groups to terrorize and humiliate freedmen and their communities. One way to achieve this was by confiscating their guns.

A SHIFT IN THINKING ON THE SECOND AMENDMENT

After the Civil War, Americans seemed to reassess the Second Amendment. The old interpretation had centered upon its relevance and urgent importance to the arming of local militias. Now, the universal right to bear arms was being tested by states attempting to strip freedmen of their Second Amendment rights. Fear of armed African Americans overshadowed anxiety over a poorly equipped and unready local militia. As Yale professor Akhil Reed Amar notes, "In short, between 1775 and 1866, the poster boy of arms morphed from the Concord Minuteman to the Carolina freedman."

THE FOURTEENTH AMENDMENT

In response to Southern civil rights violations, John Bingham, a lawyer and U.S. Representative from Ohio who had investigated the assassination of Abraham

Lincoln, decided to take more forceful legal action to protect the constitutional rights of African Americans.

In 1865, Bingham began drafting a new constitutional amendment, which, among other things, would declare all African Americans full-fledged American citizens. As quoted by Adam Winkler in a 2011 issue of the *Atlantic*, Bingham believed that the Southern "black codes," defended by Southerners as an expression of states' rights, had turned the Constitution, "a sublime and beautiful scripture, into a horrid charter of wrong."

Bingham also stated that all "privileges or immunities" of citizenship, as enjoyed by all American citizens, could not be abridged. Supporters hoped this would clarify that African Americans could not be forcibly disarmed, whether by mob violence or by the state, because bearing arms was such a crucial and fundamental constitutional right. Bingham's proposed amendment was explicitly directed at the states, especially those of the former Confederacy. The provision, ratified as part of Section 1 of the Fourteenth Amendment in 1868, reads:

No State shall make or enforce any law which shall abridge the privileges or immunities of citizens of the

United States; nor shall any State deprive any person of life, liberty, or property, without due process of law; nor deny to any person within its jurisdiction the equal protection of the laws.

UNITED STATES V. CRUIKSHANK (1875)

One important Second Amendment case arose out of an election dispute in Grant Parish, Louisiana, in 1872. Black Republican freedmen, angry over their harassment at the polls and voter fraud, which resulted in a white victory in a majority black area, marched to the courthouse in the county seat, Colfax. They occupied the building but were later overwhelmed by three hundred armed white men. Most of the African Americans were unarmed, but somewhere between 100 to 280 of them lost their lives, most of them murdered after having surrendered to the mob. Only three white men were killed.

When the state of Louisiana refused to press charges against the white mob, the federal government stepped in and indicted one of the ringleaders, cotton planter Bill Cruikshank, along with ninety-three others. They were charged with murder and conspiracy to deny the black victims their civil rights. Cruikshank and two others were convicted of conspiracy. They

THE BIRTH OF THE NRA

The most influential organization in the history of the American gun debate—the National Rifle Association (NRA)—was founded in 1871. Union army veterans General George Wood Wingate and William Conant Church, editor of the *Army and Navy Journal*, initially started the NRA to help improve the marksmanship of American soldiers and shooting hobbyists.

Unlike the modern NRA, which fiercely opposes almost all gun control and declares the defense of the Second Amendment as its main organizing principle, the NRA of the nineteenth century concentrated on firearms training rather than politics. Its motto until 1977 was "Firearms Safety Education, Marksmanship Training, Shooting for Recreation."

In its early days, the NRA interpreted the Second Amendment in terms of its bearing on local militias. It believed all citizens should be well trained in case of emergencies, such as foreign invasion or domestic disturbances like Shays' Rebellion. In fact, in the decades after its founding, the NRA led gun control and regulation efforts, helping write much of the relevant legislation—laws that today's NRA would likely oppose at every step.

appealed, and their case eventually reached the Supreme Court. Cruikshank's defense against his federal conviction rested on his claim that the federal government had no authority to convict in this instance.

Ultimately, the Supreme Court declared that it had no authority over the case because the Fourteenth Amendment only restricted abuses at the federal level. It affirmed that if no infringement by Congress could be found, then it could not rule on Cruikshank's guilt or innocence. Congress had not infringed on the rights of the victims—that was Cruikshank's doing. Indirectly, the Court was declaring that states had precedence in certain matters.

Two of the amendments in question in this decision were the First and Second. Government prosecutors argued that Cruikshank and his cohorts had denied their victims their First Amendment rights by preventing their efforts to "peaceably assemble." Their Second Amendment rights had been violated because they were unable to gain access to firearms as black men and therefore could not adequately defend themselves from the murderous mob of armed white men. However, the Court said that it was the states' job to prosecute capital crimes (like murder and manslaughter) and most civil rights infringements, including violations of the First and Second Amendments. The ruling also swung the courts back to the militia-based interpretation of the Second Amendment and away from the individual right to bear arms.

This "dual citizenship" concept—in which different rights applied to the individual on the state and federal level—would impact the rights of blacks for many decades. For them, dual citizenship meant their right of self-defense and bearing firearms would be determined by the whims of the states and not by constitutional mandates. The *Cruikshank* precedent would also prevent meaningful civil rights legislation for most of the next century.

PRESSER V. ILLINOIS (1886)

Another legal challenge regarding the Second Amendment came in Illinois in 1886. Herman Presser, a German American, had marched at the head of the Lehr und Wehr Verein (Instruct and Defend Association), a local militia, in the streets of Chicago in 1879. Presser and others had ties to the Socialist Labor Party and had formed the militia to oppose the private security forces hired by his membership's employers. An Illinois court tried Presser for setting up an illegal militia, claiming that only ones with official sanction or license from the governor of Illinois or the U.S.

military were permitted. He pled not guilty, yet was convicted and had to pay a $10 fine.

Presser appealed, and his case later reached the Supreme Court. At issue was whether states could regulate and restrict "private armies"—in other words, private militias. Presser claimed that his actions were protected under the Second Amendment.

The Supreme Court disagreed. In line with *Cruikshank*, it reaffirmed that states had the authority to regulate militias and similar groups. The opinion stated, "We think it clear that the sections under consideration, which only forbid bodies of men to associate together as military organizations, or to drill or parade with arms in cities and towns unless authorized by law, do not infringe the right of the people to keep and bear arms."

While the Court did affirm that states are limited in their powers to restrict firearms and militias, it only said that states may not disarm the populace to the point where they cannot successfully organize a needed militia in times of emergency. Private militias could be outlawed by the states, and many states did in fact have such regulations on their books. Again, the Court declared that while Congress cannot impose such restrictions, the states can do so at their discretion, within limits.

State senator and New York City political boss Timothy "Big Tim" Sullivan (*center*) helped pass what is now one of the oldest existing anti-gun measures in U.S. history.

associated with the Mafia perpetrators operating within their communities.

Only five state senators voted against the Sullivan Act. Another controversy surrounded so-called "may issue" restrictions. Rather than simply require a standard procedure for licensing guns ("shall issue"), gun licenses were issued only with the approval of the New York Police Department. Many other states soon followed New York, including Oregon in 1913, which also prohibited handgun purchases without licenses. Gun control soon became a fact of life nationwide.

PROHIBITION, GANGSTERS, AND OUTLAWS

Much as militias and gun rights were previously seen as state issues, lawmakers still saw crime as a local issue. However, organized crime networks had established an interstate reach. Law enforcement remained behind the times. Until the 1920s, there was little political will to involve the federal government in crime-fighting.

Meanwhile, the gangsters and other criminals on America's streets were able to afford incredibly powerful weaponry with money earned from bootlegging (smuggling and selling illegal alcohol) and other rackets, or crimes. This same wealth allowed criminals to bribe corrupt politicians and police, preventing cities from truly fighting crime.

Newspapers and radio broadcasts brought home to Americans the bloody turf wars on the streets. By the 1930s, pressure mounted for the federal government to take action. Some historians believe that 1929's St. Valentine's Day Massacre in Chicago was the tipping point. Gangsters likely employed by infamous Chicago boss Al Capone executed seven men with division, the National Revolver Association, proposed laws that punished the use of firearms in the commission of crimes, required permits for concealed weapons, and barred non-U.S. citizens from owning handguns. The NRA even supported a waiting period for purchasers and a requirement that gun dealers inform police of purchasing activity.

Public outcry over gun violence was widespread, and gun control measures were therefore popular. Whether these new laws and regulations infringed upon the Second Amendment was a question largely ignored at the time. Rather than being controversial, gun control was considered a reasonable, rational, and responsible response to gun-related crime and violence.

UNITED STATES V. MILLER (1939)

The 1930s and the 1940s marked growing federal power in firearms regulation. Gun enthusiasts and dealers often resented the new laws. It was the interstate transport of firearms that refocused judicial and public attention on the Second Amendment.

In 1938, Jack Miller and Frank Layton were charged with carrying an unregistered sawed-off shotgun across state lines, from Oklahoma to Arkansas. The gun did not bear the required tax stamp. The Arkansas District Court agreed with the defendants that the NFA was likely unconstitutional, throwing out their indictment. Justice Hearsill Ragon wrote in his opinion, "The court is of the opinion that this section is invalid, in that it violates the Second Amendment to the Constitution of the United States." The stage was set for the Supreme Court's first challenge to recent congressional gun control.

THE U.S. GOVERNMENT APPEALS

In challenging the lower court's ruling, the U.S. government was playing a high-stakes game. While Arkansas' ruling did not truly affect how the new federal legislation would play elsewhere, a "domino effect" was possible. Miller's victory could inspire others to challenge all gun control laws.

The U.S. government argued several points before the Supreme Court. One claim was that the NFA was mainly a tax regulation and thus legal under the authority of the Internal Revenue Service (IRS). It also claimed that since the defendants had moved guns across state lines, their criminal actions fell under federal authority.

In addition, federal lawyers directly challenged Arkansas' interpretation of the Second Amendment, saying that it only applied to guns that might be used the 1970s, many blacks and Latinos embraced gun control measures, too, as a means of increasing their personal safety and the safety of their streets and neighborhoods.

GUNS FOR SPORT AND LEISURE

Although the fear of "the wrong people" getting their hands on firearms was strong, guns remained a prized possession for many Americans. This was and remains

Sport shooting and other gun-related activities are a cherished family tradition for many Americans—even a way of life. Many honest citizens feel threatened by gun control.

especially true for sport shooters and hunters, many of whom live outside America's heavily populated urban centers.

Lawmakers wanted to ensure that the new laws did not anger or infringe on the rights of law-abiding citizens—in other words, those who obtained guns for "legitimate," noncriminal purposes. These included hunters, sport shooters, those with special permits because of their line of work, or simply those who wanted to keep a gun at home for self-defense.

For hunters, hobbyists, and others, firearms were thus subjected to the "sporting purposes" standard under the GCA. This limited firearm imports to guns that could be used for hunting, competitive target shooting, and similar shooting sports. Other exceptions for nonsporting purposes were made with special applications.

The GCA thus banned the import of foreign-made assault rifles and machine guns. Some criticized this part of the law because domestic versions that were virtually identical to the illegal foreign imports were still allowed in many cases. Thus some lawmakers believed the law was ineffective—just a cosmetic rule that, in the end, did not constitute an honest effort to stop gun violence and crime.

The end result was the Firearm Owners Protection Act of 1986 (FOPA). Two dozen modifications were made to the earlier law. These included the lifting of a ban on interstate ammunition sales and a relaxing of the rule banning mail-order firearms. It also allowed dealers to sell weapons at gun shows and lifted certain restrictions on transporting firearms interstate.

THE NEW FAR RIGHT: ARMED AND DANGEROUS

Many conservatives from the American heartland have grown mistrustful of the federal government and fear the death of the Second Amendment. They are suspicious of federal law enforcement, including the FBI and especially the ATF, which they fear and resent because of its oversight of firearms.

Extremists have given mainstream hobbyists and gun rights advocates a bad name. Some have belonged to far-right and white supremacist groups such as the Ku Klux Klan, and the no-longer-operational Order, whose members robbed banks and committed murders in the Midwest. Others belong to neo-Nazi organizations. Still others stockpile guns as part of apocalyptic (end-of-the-world) cults that predict a final showdown with the federal government, which they consider to be a satanic agent of evil.

Representative William J. Hughes inserted a controversial addition to FOPA. The Hughes Amendment banned the sale of fully automatic machine guns that were made after May 19, 1986. The amendment also placed some restrictions on the exchange of guns made before that date. While some parts of FOPA appealed to gun rights advocates, many gun owners wanted the Hughes Amendment repealed. They said that few crimes involved machine guns and that, therefore, the law merely criminalized innocent collectors and hobbyists.

THE WACO SIEGE

After President Bill Clinton took office, one extremist group, the Branch Davidians, a religious sect based in Waco, Texas, faced off with the ATF, the FBI, and the Texas National Guard between February and April 1993. Suspected of stockpiling illegal weapons, the Branch Davidians engaged in a tense standoff that was broadcast on American television for weeks. An early raid was repelled by the group and its leader, David Koresh. Finally, on April 19, a fire started as federal agents stormed the Branch Davidian compound a second time. In all, four federal agents and seventy-six members of the sect perished, including children.

This April 1995 photo shows the Alfred P. Murrah Federal Building in Oklahoma City after its bombing. The event intensified the debate between pro- and anti-gun forces.

When Timothy McVeigh blew up the Alfred P. Murrah Federal Building on April 19, 1995, in Oklahoma City, Oklahoma, killing 168 people (including young children), he said that Waco was a primary motivation for his own plot. The deadliest terrorist attack on U.S. soil until September 11, 2001, the Oklahoma City bombing was a frightening indicator of the growing anger in some sectors of the population against the federal government.

Gun control advocates were furious, claiming that NRA rhetoric had contributed to a dangerous, anti-government atmosphere. Wayne LaPierre, executive vice president and chief executive officer of the NRA, had sent out a fund-raising letter a few days before the Oklahoma bombing. It described federal agents as "jack-booted government thugs...[with] Nazi bucket helmets and black storm trooper uniforms." Former U.S. president George H.W. Bush resigned his NRA membership in protest.

THE DEEP DIVIDE: "GUN NUTS" VS. "GUN GRABBERS"

Perhaps no single event during the Clinton years split the pro- and anti-gun control camps as much as the Waco siege. Each side saw Waco and similar events in an entirely different light. Second Amendment activists viewed the Waco raid as clear evidence that private citizens could be harassed for their religious beliefs by the federal government and killed for their resistance. As Adam Winkler writes in *Gun Fight*, "Law enforcement was demonized as the enemy, prone to abusive behavior and disregard for the rights of the people." For them, Washington, D.C., might as well have been as far off as England was from the thirteen colonies.

Gun control advocates, however, considered this line of reasoning to be hysterical and unhinged and viewed its proponents as paranoid "gun nuts." They saw groups like the Branch Davidians as filled with dangerous and unbalanced extremists who should be prevented from having weapons at all. They believed that legislation could and should stop them from committing violent, antisocial acts. Their gun rights opponents, in turn, saw them as "gun grabbers."

THE CLINTON YEARS: GUN CONTROL VICTORIES

Years after Jim and Sarah Brady first proposed it, the Brady Handgun Violence Protection Act finally passed in November 1993. It was considered a major victory for gun control advocates. The act instituted a five-day waiting period and mandatory background checks for handgun buyers, which took effect in February 1994. Brady and his wife would remain active in gun control efforts for years to come.

The NRA launched a legal challenge to the act as an infringement on states' rights. Wayne LaPierre initially endorsed instant background checks, but the NRA pressed for the whole statute to be voided. In

An illustration shows how rounds fit into the magazine of a Glock 19 semiautomatic pistol. Many gun control advocates argue that such weapons should be restricted to law enforcement.

Printz v. United States, the Supreme Court did not decide on the constitutionality of background checks. It did declare, however, that states could not be forced by the federal government to conduct background checks.

An officer patrols Oakland Technical High School on December 17, 2012, three days after the Sandy Hook shooting. Gun rights advocates favored beefing up security over regulation as a solution.

"gun grabbers" want to ban all guns for everyone but members of the military, police, and certain professions (such as security guards).

Meanwhile, hardcore gun rights advocates insist that more guns are the solution, not fewer. School shootings would happen less frequently, they argue, if shooters knew that school staff members—and, on college campuses, the students—were armed. They assert that a well-armed populace could fight fire with fire, kill the rogue shooters, and ultimately save lives. Furthermore, they argue that crime in general would decline if criminals knew that robbing someone or breaking into their home would put them at risk of being gunned down by armed citizens.

THE "GUN SHOW LOOPHOLE"

After the Columbine massacre, Democrats acted quickly to amend previous laws to mandate background checks on all gun purchasers. This would theoretically fix something mistakenly called the "gun show loophole." Under current laws, unlicensed sellers could perform private sales without the background checks required of federally licensed dealers. Many such sales occurred at gun shows, hence the name. Senator Charles Schumer of New York declared, according to the *Los Angeles Times*, "It will never be the same again. The vise lock that the NRA has had on the Senate and the House is broken." The measure failed, however, and little really changed. The measures taken by local communities and states were extensive, but no federal legislation truly made an impact on how guns were regulated.

Their opponents counter that we should discourage gun ownership in society. They also point out that mentally disturbed individuals rarely consider or care about their own safety when going on a shooting rampage. In fact, they typically hope and plan to die during their rampage. Whether or not victims are potentially armed in these circumstances would therefore have no deterrent effect upon a would-be attacker.

THE VIRGINIA TECH MASSACRE

In 2007, society was once again divided on the easy availability of powerful firearms. Seung-Hui Cho, a student at Virginia Polytechnic Institute and State University (Virginia Tech) in Blacksburg, Virginia, went on a rampage on his school campus. In the course of a few hours, Cho, who had been previously diagnosed with severe anxiety disorder, killed thirty-two people, including faculty and students. Seventeen others were wounded. It remains the deadliest massacre by a single gunman in U.S. history.

Observers worldwide blamed American gun culture and lax regulation of gun purchasing, registration, and ownership. Critics asked how Cho was able to procure guns despite the supposed safeguards in place with the National Instant Criminal Background Check

Disturbing images sent by Virginia Tech shooter Seung-Hui Cho surfaced after his death on national television, including this one of Cho brandishing his Walther and Glock semiautomatic pistols (courtesy of http://www.zumapress.com/zpdtl.html?IMG-200704 18_kil_z0...).

System (NICS). The NRA and gun owners went on the offensive, too. They blamed a deficient mental health care system and the university itself for not noticing Cho's warning signs. He had been erratic and intimidating both in class and with fellow dorm mates. According to the NRA, Cho was obviously a loose cannon waiting to explode.

Despite misgivings, the NRA cooperated with its rivals in the wake of the Virginia Tech massacre. Perhaps because it did not directly put restrictions on weapons, the NICS Improvement Amendments Act of 2007 was supported by the NRA, in conjunction with the pro-gun control Brady Campaign. The death toll at Virginia Tech was so large, the scenario so frightening, that few opposed the modest measures proposed by the act. These included mandatory improvements in how states report and track "prohibited persons" such as the mentally ill, criminals, and others deemed too dangerous to own firearms.

SHOWDOWN: *DISTRICT OF COLUMBIA V. HELLER* (2008)

The Supreme Court took on another crucial Second Amendment case in 2008. It was the first one to directly address the individual right to keep and bear arms for self-defense. The gun regulations in question were those of Washington, D.C. The city had the strictest restrictions in the nation—even self-defense with legally registered rifles and shotguns was not protected.

The landmark case arose out of several earlier local and appeals court cases that rose all the way up to the Supreme Court. D.C. police officer Dick Heller wanted

Dick Heller gives a thumbs-up at a Washington, D.C., police precinct in August 2008, while holding his gun permit. He won the right to bear arms in his Supreme Court case.

to keep a gun at home. This was prohibited, even though Heller was allowed to carry firearms on the job. He felt unsafe living near a housing complex overrun with drugs and crime. Heller's lawyers pressed the Supreme Court to finally make a solid, definitive decision on whether or not the Second Amendment guaranteed the individual right to bear arms for self-defense and personal protection.

The Court's decision was a major gun rights victory. Justin Antonin Scalia, writing for the majority opinion, declared that the Second Amendment "protects an individual right to possess a firearm unconnected with service in a militia, and to use that arm for traditionally lawful purposes, such as self-defense within the home." Thus, banning handguns in this case violated a natural, constitutional right to bear arms. Another measure, which required a trigger lock or disassembly (taking apart) of the gun if it were in the home, was also declared unconstitutional because it would prevent a person from using the weapon in a sudden emergency.

MCDONALD V. CHICAGO (2010)

The next battleground Supreme Court case occurred in 2010. This time, the Court's decision would go beyond federal regulations. The plaintiff, seventy-six-year-old retiree Otis McDonald, was concerned about his neighborhood being overrun by the drug trade. Having experienced several break-ins, he feared for his safety. McDonald was a hunter with legally registered shotguns, which he kept at home. He wanted a hand-gun, however, because he felt the larger guns would be inconvenient in the event of an emergency—a home invasion, for example.

However, the Chicago ordinance prohibited any-one from owning "any firearm unless such person is the holder of a valid registration certificate for such firearm." Together with a citywide ban on handgun registration that went into effect in 1982, the city's combined gun laws effectively banned handguns for any Chicago resident. McDonald and two other Chicagoans challenged the rule in court, and the lawsuit rose to the U.S. Court of Appeals for the 7th Circuit and from there to the Supreme Court. The argument in the *McDonald* case was based on the idea that the Court must declare the right to bear arms (without invasive or onerous restrictions) to be a "fundamental" right, like that of free speech. In this case, the Supreme Court decided that it was.

The Court declared that the "Second Amendment protects the right to possess a handgun in the home for the purpose of self-defense [...] A provision of the Bill of Rights that protects a right that is fundamental from an American perspective applies equally to the Federal Government and the States. We therefore hold that the Due Process Clause of the Fourteenth Amendment incorporates the Second Amendment right recognized in *Heller*." The U.S. Constitution's due process clause provides a safeguard from arbitrary denial of life, liberty, or property by the government outside the sanction of law. Added Justice Samuel Alito, "The Fourteenth Amendment makes the Second Amendment right to keep and bear arms fully applicable to the States."

Chicago Mayor Richard Daley, a Democrat, told the *New York Times* that the ruling could make his city's gun laws unenforceable, adding, "Across the country, cities are struggling with how to address this issue…Common sense tells you we need fewer guns on the street, not more guns."

ANOTHER NATIONAL TRAGEDY: SANDY HOOK

Since Virginia Tech, there have been more mass shootings, including the shocking 2013 attack on the Washington Navy Yard by Aaron Alexis, an emotionally disturbed navy reservist, who gunned down twelve base workers and wounded several others. However, the Sandy Hook Massacre in Connecticut in December 2012 was an eruption of gun violence that profoundly shook Americans and raised new doubts about the extent of Second Amendment rights and protections.

A troubled young man, Adam Lanza, killed his mother at their home, then drove to his former

A New England Patriots fan shows her support for the victims and families of the Sandy Hook shooting during a game on December 16, 2012.

The NFA is an organization of Canadian gun owners that pushes for gun rights and keeps its members informed about their right to bear arms under Canadian law.

Canadian Firearms Program
RCMP National Headquarters
73 Leikin Drive
Ottawa, ON K1A 0R2
Canada
(613) 993-7267
Web site: http://www.rcmp-grc.gc.ca/cfp-pcaf/index-eng.htm
The Canadian Firearms Program is administered by the Royal Canadian Mounted Police. It tracks and combats illegal firearms and maintains a registry program for gun owners.

Center for Gun Policy and Research
John Hopkins Bloomberg School of Public Health
John Hopkins University
615 N. Wolfe Street
Baltimore, MD 21205
(410) 516-8000
Web site: http://www.jhsph.edu/research/centers-and-institutes/johns-hopkins-center-for-gun-policy-and-research

The Center for Gun Policy and Research is dedicated to bringing objective and informative academic research to enhance American legislative policy-making and reduce gun violence.

Coalition to Stop Gun Violence (CSGV)
1424 L Street NW, Suite 2-1
Washington, DC 20005
(202) 408-0061
Web site: http://www.csgv.org
The CSGV is a nonprofit organization that conducts research about and advocates against gun violence. It is comprised of dozens of local and regional gun control groups.

Liberty Belles
P.O. Box 3631
Salem, OR 97302
Web site: http://www.libertybelles.org
Liberty Belles is a pro-Second Amendment nonprofit organization with a focus on empowering women to defend their right to bear arms.

National Rifle Association of America (NRA)
11250 Waples Mill Road
Fairfax, VA 22030
(800) 672-3888

Web site: http:// http://programs.nra.org

The NRA is the premier gun rights lobby in the
    United States. It also runs programs for sport
    shooting and other gun-related activities.

Supreme Court of the United States

1 First Street NE

Washington, DC 20543

Web site: http://www.supremecourt.gov

The Supreme Court is the nation's highest court and is
    responsible for deciding whether laws and legisla-
    tion comply properly with the U.S. Constitution.

WEB SITES

Due to the changing nature of Internet links, Rosen
Publishing has developed an online list of Web sites
related to the subject of this book. This site is updated
regularly. Please use this link to access the list:

http://www.rosenlinks.com/UUSC/Gun

FOR FURTHER READING

Barton, David. *The Second Amendment*. Aledo, TX: Wallbuilder Press, 2000.

Charles, Patrick J. *The Second Amendment: The Intent and Its Interpretation by the States and the Supreme Court*. Jefferson, NC: McFarland & Company, 2009.

Cornell, Saul. *A Well-Regulated Militia: The Founding Fathers and the Origins of Gun Control in America*. New York, NY: Oxford University Press, 2008.

Cross, Nathaniel, and Michael A. Sommers. *Understanding Your Right to Bear Arms* (Personal Freedom & Civic Duty). New York, NY: Rosen Publishing, 2011.

Gerber, Larry. *The Second Amendment: The Right to Bear Arms* (Amendments to the United States Constitution: The Bill of Rights). New York, NY: Rosen Publishing, 2011.

Gerdes, Louise. *Gun Violence* (Opposing Viewpoints). New York, NY: Greenhaven Press, 2010.

Henigan, Dennis A. *Lethal Logic: Exploding the Myths That Paralyze American Gun Policy*. Dulles, VA: Potomac Books, 2009.

Kellner, Douglas. *Guys and Guns Amok: Domestic Terrorism and School Shootings from the Oklahoma City Bombing to the Virginia Tech*

Massacre (Radical Imagination Series). Boulder, CO: Paradigm Publishers, 2008.

LaPierre, Wayne. *Guns, Freedom, & Terrorism*. New York, NY: Liberty Library/Smashwords, 2011.

Lott, John R., Jr. *More Guns, Less Crime: Understanding Crime and Gun Control Laws*, (Studies in Law and Economics). 3rd ed. Chicago, IL: University of Chicago Press, 2010.

MacKay, Jenny. *The Columbine School Shootings* (Crime Scene Investigations). San Diego, CA: Lucent Books, 2010.

MacKay, Jenny. *Gun Control* (Hot Topics). New York, NY: Lucent Books, 2013.

Merino, Noel. *Gun Control* (Introducing Issues with Opposing Viewpoints). New York, NY: Greenhaven Press, 2012.

Roleff, Tamara. *Gun Control* (Opposing Viewpoints). New York, NY: Greenhaven Press, 2007.

Smith, Rich. *Second and Third Amendments: The Right to Security* (Bill of Rights). Minneapolis, MN: ABDO & Daughters, 2007.

Spitzer, Robert J. *The Politics of Gun Control*. 5th ed. Boulder, CO: Paradigm Publishers, 2012.

Valdez, Angela. *Gun Control* (Point/Counterpoint). New York, NY: Chelsea House, 2011.

Watkins, Christine. *Guns and Crime* (At Issue Series). New York, NY: Greenhaven Press, 2012.

Whitney, Craig. *Living with Guns: A Liberal's Case for the Second Amendment.* New York, NY: PublicAffairs Books, 2012.

Worth, Richard. *Massacre at Virginia Tech: Disaster & Survival* (Deadly Disasters). Berkeley Heights, NJ: Enslow Publishers, 2008.

BIBLIOGRAPHY

Ames, Mark. *Going Postal: Rage, Murder, and Rebellion—From Reagan's Workplaces to Clinton's Columbine and Beyond*. New York, NY: Soft Skull Press, 2005.

Chew, Cassie M. "The Assault Weapons Ban as Understood by a 2nd Amendment Scholar." *PBS Newshour*, March 21, 2013. Retrieved July 2013 (http://www.pbs.org/newshour/rundown/2013/03/the-assault-weapons-ban-as-understood-by-a-second-amendment-scholar.html).

Cornell, Saul. "Gun-Rights Advocates Should Fear History of Second Amendment." *Daily Beast*, December 18, 2012. Retrieved September 2013 (http://www.thedailybeast.com/articles/2012/12/18/gun-rights-advocates-should-fear-history-of-second-amendment.html).

Cornell, Saul. "The Second Amendment You Don't Know." *New York Daily News*, December 19, 2012. Retrieved July 2013 (http://www.nydailynews.com/opinion/amendment-don-article-1.1223900).

Duffy, Peter. "100 Years Ago, the Shot That Spurred New York's Gun-Control Law." *New York Times*, January 23, 2011. Retrieved July 2013 (http://cityroom.blogs.nytimes.com/2011/01/23/100-years-ago-the-shot-that-spurred-new-yorks-gun-control-law/?_r=0).

Good, Chris. "Interview: Brady Campaign President Paul Helmke on Why the Gun Ruling Isn't So Bad." *Atlantic*, June 28, 2010. Retrieved August 2013 (http://www.theatlantic.com/politics/ archive/2010/06/interview-brady-campaign-president-paul-helmke-on-why-the-gun-ruling-isnt-so-bad/58849).

Jackson, Allison. "NRA Breaks Its Silence Over Sandy Hook Mass Shooting in Newtown, Connecticut." *Global Post*, December 18, 2012. Retrieved July 2013 (http://www.globalpost.com/dispatch/news /regions/americas/united-states/121218/nra-breaks-silence-over-sandy-hook-mass-shooting-Newtown-Connecticut).

Kornacki, Steve. "When Democrats Won on Guns." Salon.com, December 17, 2012. Retrieved July 2013 (http://www.salon.com/2012/12/17/when_democrats_won_on_guns).

Lee, Jack. "10 Surprising Facts About the NRA That You Never Hear." Policymic.com, January 2013. Retrieve July 2013 (http://www.policymic.com /articles/23929/10-surprising-facts-about-the-nra-that-you-never-hear).

Lind, Michael. "Guns Have Never Saved Us." Salon. com, December 17, 2012. Retrieved July 2013 (http://www.salon.com/2012/12/17/guns_have_never_saved_us).

Lind, Michael. "The Secret History of the Bill of Rights." Salon.com, June 20, 2013. Retrieved July 2013 (http://www.salon.com/2013/06/20/the_secret_history_of_the_bill_of_rights).

Liptak, Adam. "Justices Extend Firearms Rights in 5-to-4 Ruling." *New York Times*, June 28, 2010. Retrieved August 2013 (http://www.nytimes.com/2010/06/29/us/29scotus.html?_r=0).

Malcolm, Joyce Lee. "Two Cautionary Tales of Gun Control." *Wall Street Journal*, December 26, 2012. Retrieved December 2012 (http://online.wsj.com/article/SB10001424127887323777204578195470446855466.html).

Mason, Melanie. "Attempt to Close Gun Show Loophole Has Failed Before." *Los Angeles Times*, February 26, 2013. Retrieved July 2013 (http://articles.latimes.com/2013/feb/26/nation/la-na-gunshow-loophole-20130226).

PBS.org. "Need to Know: PBS: Debating the Second Amendment, Roundtable Participants." April 26, 2013. Retrieved July 2013 (http://www.pbs.org/wnet/need-to-know/politics-3/debating-the-second-amendment-roundtable-participants/16832).

Pew Charitable Trusts. "Gun Actions Since Sandy Hook Shooting." June 13, 2013. Retrieved August 2013 (http://www.pewstates.org/research/data-visualizations/gun-actions-since-sandy-hook-shooting-85899482178).

Raffin, Ross. "Mason, Madison, and Militias: A Progressive for a Right to Bear Arms." *Stanford Progressive*, May 2010. Retrieved July 2013 (http://www.stanford.edu/group/progressive/cgi-bin/?p=559).

Rosenfeld, Steven. "The Surprising Unknown History of the NRA." Alternet.org, January 13, 2013. Retrieved July 2013 (http://www.alternet.org/suprising-unknown-history-nra).

Shen, Aviva. "What We've Learned in the 14 Years Since the Columbine Shooting." ThinkProgress.org, April 20, 2013. Retrieved July 2013 (http://thinkprogress.org/politics/2013/04/20/1896851/what-weve-learned-in-the-14-years-since-the-columbine-shooting).

Sweeney, Kevin, and Saul Cornell. "All Guns Are Not Created Equal." *Chronicle of Higher Education*, January 28, 2013. Retrieved August 2013 (http://chronicle.com/article/All-Guns-Are-Not-Created-Equal/136805).

TheTakeaway.org/WNYC Radio. "A Liberal's Case for Guns." December 17, 2012. Retrieved July 2013 (http://www.thetakeaway.org/2012/dec/17/gun-control-debate-begins-wake-newtown-shooting).

Vandercoy, David E. "The History of the Second Amendment." *Valparaiso University Law Review*, 1994. Retrieved August 2013 (http://www.constitution.org/2ll/2ndschol/89vand.pdf).

Weisman, Jonathan. "Senate Blocks Drive for Gun Control." *New York Times*, April 17, 2013. Retrieved August 2013 (http://www.nytimes.com/2013/04/18/us/politics/senate-obama-gun-control.html?pagewanted=all&_r=0).

Welch, William M. "Effects of Assassination Attempt on Reagan Echo Today." *USA Today*, January 24, 2011. Retrieved August 2013 (http://usatoday30.usatoday.com/news/washington/2011-01-23-ronald-reagan-assassination-attempt-effect_N.htm).

Winkler, Adam. *Gun Fight: The Battle Over the Right to Bear Arms in America*. New York, NY: W. W. Norton and & Company, 2011.

Winkler, Adam. "The Secret History of Guns." *Atlantic*, July 24, 2011. Retrieved July 2013 (http://www.theatlantic.com/magazine/archive/2011/09/the-secret-history-of-guns/308608).

INDEX

ABOUT THE AUTHOR

Philip Wolny is a writer and editor from New York City. His other gun-related titles for Rosen include books on hunting, hunting safety, and military issues.

PHOTO CREDITS

Cover George Frey/Getty Images; p. 3 spirit of america /Shutterstock.com; pp. 4, 65 Karen Bleier/AFP/Getty Images; pp. 7, 20, 36, 48, 63, 78 Mikhail Kolesnikov /Shutterstock.com; pp. 8–9, 11 SuperStock; p. 15 cass greene/E+/Getty Images; p. 17 Visions of America/ SuperStock; p. 21 Hulton Archive/Getty Images; pp. 24–25, 27, 39 Library of Congress Prints and Photographs Division; p. 37 Chicago History Museum /Archive Photos/Getty Images; p. 42 Popperfoto/Getty Images; p. 49 Mondadori/Getty Images; p. 52 Bentley Archive/Popperfoto/Getty Images; pp. 54–55 MPI /Archive Photos/Getty Images; pp. 58, 81 © AP Images; p. 61 Ryan Houston/Flickr Vision/Getty Images; p. 68 Dirck Halstead//Time & Life Pictures/Getty Images; p. 70 Robert Llewellyn/Photolibrary/Getty Images; p. 73 Bob Daemmerich/AFP/Getty Images; p. 76 McClatchy-Tribune/Getty Images; p. 79 Bloomberg/Getty Images; p. 84 © MSNBC/ZUMA Press; p. 86 Mark Wilson/Getty Images; pp. 90–91 Jim Rogash/Getty Images; cover and interior design elements: design36/Shutterstock.com, Eky Studio/Shutterstock.com, Flame of life/Shutterstock .com, Brandon Bourdages/Shutterstock.com; back cover (constitution detail) J. Helgason/Shutterstock.com.

Designer: Michael Moy; Editor: Heather Moore Niver; Photo researcher: Amy Feinberg